A Guide for Using

The Mouse and the Motorcycle

in the Classroom

Property Of Kymberlee E. Reels

Based on the novel written by Beverly Cleary

This guide written by **Deborah Shepherd Hayes**

Teacher Created Materials, Inc.
6421 Industry Way
Westminster, CA 92683
www.teachercreated.com
©*1995 Teacher Created Materials*
Reprinted, 2003
Made in U.S.A.
ISBN 1-55734-529-5

Illustrated by
José L. Tapia

Edited by
Judith Brewer

Cover Art by
Wendy Chang

Table of Contents

- ❖ Quiz Time
- ❖ Hands-On Project—Motorcycle Madness
- ❖ Cooperative Learning Activity—Measuring Up
- ❖ Curriculum Connection—Plot a Course
- ❖ Into Your Life—Reading Response Journals

- ❖ Quiz Time
- ❖ Hands-On Project—Racer Ralph
- ❖ Cooperative Learning Activity—Workin' the Line
- ❖ Curriculum Connection—A Flash of History
- ❖ Into Your Life—The DMV and You

- ❖ Quiz Time
- ❖ Hands-On Project—Crash Helmet
- ❖ Cooperative Learning Activity—Designing Your School Menu
- ❖ Curriculum Connection—Famous Mice. . . Mouse Von Trapp?
- ❖ Into Your Life—It's All in the Family

- ❖ Quiz Time
- ❖ Hands-On Project—Dress the Part
- ❖ Cooperative Learning Activity—Laughable Limericks
- ❖ Curriculum Connection—Acids, Neutrals, and Covering Your Bases
- ❖ Into Your Life—The Pet Shop

- ❖ Quiz Time
- ❖ Hands-On Project—Ralph's Adventure Map
- ❖ Cooperative Learning Activity—Readers' Theater
- ❖ Curriculum Connection—Dem Bones
- ❖ Into Your Life—Be Our Guest

Introduction

A good book can touch our lives like a good friend. Within its pages are words and characters that can inspire us to achieve our highest ideals. We can turn to it for companionship, recreation, comfort, and guidance. It also gives us a cherished story to hold in our hearts forever.

In *Literature Units*, great care has been taken to select books that are sure to become good friends!

Teachers who use this literature unit will find the following features to supplement their own valuable ideas:

- A Sample Lesson Plan
- Pre-reading Activities
- A Biographical Sketch and Picture of the Author
- A Book Summary
- Vocabulary Lists and Suggested Vocabulary Activities
- Chapters grouped for study, with each section including:

    – quizzes

    – hands-on projects

    – cooperative learning activities

    – cross-curriculum connections

    – extensions into the reader's own life

- Book Report Ideas
- A Culminating Activity
- Three Different Options for Unit Tests
- Bibliography of Related Reading
- Answer Key

We are confident that this unit will be a valuable addition to your planning and hope that as you use our ideas, your students will increase the circle of "friends" they can have in books!

Sample Lesson Plan

Each of the following lesson suggestions are designed to provide guidance and serve as an outline for managing the different sections of the book. Some sections can be administered in one day, while some may need an entire week for completion. Feel free to adjust this plan to your own needs.

Lesson 1

- Introduce and complete some or all of the pre-reading activities found on page 5.
- Read "About the Author" with your students. (page 6)
- Introduce vocabulary for Section 1. (page 8)
- Play a vocabulary game. (page 9)
- Have students make predictions about what the story will be about.

Lesson 2

- Review vocabulary and play a vocabulary game. (pages 8–9)
- Read Chapters 1 and 2.
- Complete the hands-on activity. (pages 11–12)
- Review measurement and do the measuring activity. (pages 13–14)
- Go over the USA map and complete the mapping activity. (page 15)
- Write in Reading Response Journals and allow time for sharing. (page 16)
- Administer the Section 1 quiz. (page 10)

Lesson 3

- Introduce the vocabulary for this section and play a vocabulary game. (pages 8–9)
- Read Chapters 3–5.
- Assemble the "Racer Ralph." (page 18)
- Work in cooperative learning groups for the assembly line activity. (page 19)
- Study the history of motorcycles. (page 20)
- Work with a partner and discover your state's DMV motorcycle laws. (page 21)
- Write in Reading Response Journals and allow time for sharing.
- Administer the Section 2 quiz. (page 17)

Lesson 4

- Review vocabulary for Sections 1 and 2. (page 8)
- Introduce vocabulary for Section 3 and play a vocabulary game. (pages 8–9)
- Read Chapters 6–8.
- Assemble the crash helmets. (page 23)
- Work in cooperative learning groups to design a school menu. (page 24)

- Discover some famous mice and write the before and after stories. (pages 25 and 26)
- Research family heritage and complete the family tree. (pages 27 and 28)
- Write in Reading Response Journals and allow time for sharing.
- Administer the Section 3 quiz. (page 22)

Lesson 5

- Review vocabulary for Sections 1–4. (page 8)
- Introduce vocabulary for Section 4 and play a vocabulary game. (pages 8 and 9)
- Read Chapters 9–11.
- Discuss motorcycle accessories and design Ralph's wardrobe. (page 30)
- Practice limerick writing. (page 31)
- Conduct the acids, bases, and neutrals experiment. (page 32)
- Complete the Pet Shop activity. (page 33)
- Write in Reading Response Journals and allow time for sharing.
- Administer the Section 4 quiz. (page 29)

Lesson 6

- Review vocabulary for Sections 1–4.
- Introduce vocabulary for Section 5 and play a vocabulary game. (pages 8 and 9)
- Read Chapters 12–13.
- Reconstruct Ralph's path for finding the aspirin. (page 35)
- Write scripts and perform for class in cooperative learning groups. (page 36)
- Conduct the owl pellet experiment. (page 37)
- Invite a guest speaker to your class. (page 38)
- Write in Reading Response Journals and allow time for sharing.
- Administer the Section 5 quiz. (page 34)

Lesson 7

- Review the vocabulary for the entire book and play various vocabulary games. (pages 8 and 9)
- Complete the Book Buddy Brainstorm culminating activities and share. (pages 40–42)

Lesson 8

- Assign book reports. (page 39)
- Administer Unit Tests: 1, 2, and/or 3. (pages 43–45)

Before the Book

Before you begin reading the book *The Mouse and the Motorcycle*, go to the library and check out books on mice and motorcycles. If you have access to a motorcycle repair shop, borrow a helmet and any other accessory that would make for a nice display. Once your literary corner is set up, do some pre-reading activities with the students to interest them and enhance their comprehension. Here are some activities that might work well in your class.

1. Predict what the story might be about just by hearing the title.
2. Predict what the story might be about just by looking at the cover illustration.
3. Discuss other books written by Beverly Cleary that students may have read or heard about.

   Examples:

Henry Huggins	*Runaway Ralph*
Henry and Beezuz	*Ribsy/Socks*
Ramona the Pest	*Muggie Maggie*
Ramona and Her Father	*Otis Spofford*
Ramona Quimby, Age 8	*Strider*

4. Discuss and answer these questions:

   Are you interested in . . .

   . . . stories about animals and people talking with each other?

   . . . funny stories?

   . . . stories about motorcycles?

   . . . stories about animals?

   . . . stories about friendship?

   Would you ever . . .

   . . . talk to a mouse?

   . . . risk your life to save a friend?

   . . . break a promise?

   . . . order room service?

   . . . brag to your relatives?

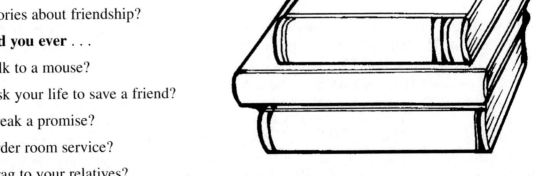

5. Using a large piece of chart paper, brainstorm everything that your class knows about mice and about motorcycles. Keep this list posted so that as the story unfolds, students can refer to their list of collective information. Locate California on a map and find Highway 40. Research the Gold Rush and old mining towns. Talk about family vacations. Create an interactive bulletin board with the "Traveling the USA" theme, using a map of the United States. Invite the students to bring in post-cards of places that they or relatives have been. Journal write about the ultimate dream vacation.

About the Author

Did you know that Beverly Cleary, one of America's most successful authors of children's literature, did not learn to read until almost the third grade? "I wept at home while my puzzled mother tried to drill me on the dreaded word charts. 'But reading is fun' insisted mother. I stamped my feet and threw the book on the floor. Reading was *not fun*."

Beverly recalls this early school experience about reading. "The first grade was sorted into three reading groups—Bluebirds, Redbirds and Blackbirds. I was a Blackbird. To be a Blackbird was to be disgraced. I wanted to read, but somehow could not."

After some practice and work, by the third grade Beverly was beginning to read successfully, but she found yet another problem. "I no longer wanted to read. . . it was boring. . . most of the stories were simplified. . . and there was no surprise left." Beverly wondered why authors could not write about the children she knew, the "plain, ordinary boys and girls." She wondered why authors did not write books that were funny.

Beverly (Bunn) Cleary was born in 1916 in McMinnville, Oregon, where she lived on a farm. She was an only child. Her father was a farmer, and her mother was a school teacher. She graduated with a Bachelor of Arts degree from the University of California, Berkeley, in 1938.

When she worked at a local library, Beverly would make up stories about a boy named Henry Huggins and his dog and would tell their adventures to the children at Saturday afternoon story hours. Eventually, she wrote the stories down, and this became the makings for her first book, *Henry and Ribsy*. This book won the Young Reader's Choice Award in 1957.

Beverly Cleary gets ideas for books in many ways, some from her own children. Her son, who was in fourth grade at the time, did not like reading, but he had a strong interest in motorcycles. This, coupled with an experience of staying in a strange hotel one vacation, led her to write *The Mouse and the Motorcycle*. This book has received a variety of awards, as well.

What this author finds most rewarding about her work is the number of people who tell her of a child who did not enjoy reading until her books came along. Struggling in school as a nonreader and finding nothing interesting about books to becoming one of the world's leading authors of children's literature is quite an accomplishment!

(direct quotes used from *Something About the Author*, Vol. 43, pp. 53–60)

The Mouse and the Motorcycle

by Beverly Cleary

(Avon, 1965)

(Available in Canada, U.K., and Australia from Al Polan, International Book Dist.)

While taking a three-week vacation across the United States, Keith Gridley and his parents ended up spending the Fourth of July at the Mountain View Inn in California. Keith's mother did not like the place from the start; it was too dusty, old, and, she felt certain, full of mice. While Keith was unpacking, Ralph, a young mouse seeking adventure, was watching him from his hole. Ralph saw Keith unpack several toy cars, one of which really got his attention—a brand new, shiny, red motorcycle! When Keith left the room, Ralph could not resist and climbed to the top of the bedside table to take it for a spin. Unfortunately, he took a spill and landed at the bottom of a metal wastebasket. This is how Keith and Ralph came to meet each other, as Keith discovered Ralph there and rescued him.

The two began talking, and Keith offered the use of his motorcycle to Ralph. Ralph was overjoyed! Keith said that Ralph could ride it at night, and he would play with it during the day. This was just the kind of adventure that Ralph was looking for! He loved the feel of the handlebars beneath his paws and the rushing wind blowing his whiskers back. Keith even offered to bring "room service" for Ralph and his family! Ralph made an unwise decision, however, when one afternoon he broke his promise to Keith and rode the motorcycle during the day. While trying to escape the powerful suction of the housekeeper's vacuum, he ended up riding into a pile of dirty linen. It was here that Ralph had to choose between quickly chewing his way out and running for his life or taking much longer to chew larger holes and take the motorcycle with him. He chose to save his life. Ralph dreaded making the confession to Keith. It was much harder to tell him because Keith had just given Ralph a special crash helmet. Keith was mad at first, but later became understanding because he knew what it was like to get into trouble too.

Meanwhile, the hotel found out about Ralph's family and declared "war on mice." During this time, Ralph's mother and relatives were in a panic and feared for their lives. Then, Keith came down with a terribly high fever. He needed an aspirin to bring the fever down, but there was none to be found. At that moment, Ralph made a very responsible and grown-up decision. Even though it was dangerous for a mouse to be seen in the hotel, Ralph decided to take the risk and search the Mountain View Inn for an aspirin. In the end, Ralph found an aspirin for Keith, thus earning his respect, as well as the respect of his mother and family. Before Keith left the hotel, he gave Ralph the motorcycle because he thought that Ralph was now old enough to own one. The two parted as good friends, and both learned many lessons about growing up.

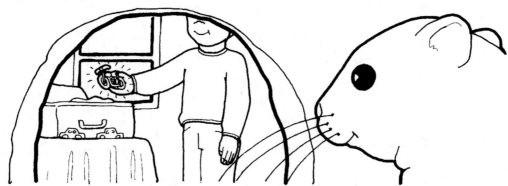

Vocabulary Lists

On this page are vocabulary lists which correspond to each sectional grouping of chapters. Vocabulary activity ideas can be found on page 9.

Section 1
(Chapters 1–2)

rumpled	threadbare	rumor
renewed	antimacassar	reckless
faucets	relenting	sensible
prevented	greedily	chromium
luggage	perplexed	quivering
chickadee	eagerly	jauntily
critically	despair	craved
interrupt	eager	scrabbled
protested	scurried	momentum
quaint	scolded	

Section 2
(Chapters 3–5)

battered	cowered	dignity
intact	protection	reassuringly
wearily	motionless	admitted
incinerator	rhythmic	sensation
remorseful	opportunity	permitted
venturing	confessed	linen
adorable	bravado	exhilarated
knothole	indignant	captive
predicament	hastily	astonished

Section 3
(Chapters 6–8)

nuisance	boasting	revealing
chastened	admiring	genuinely
astounded	devour	pilfering
incredulous	avoid	foolhardy
occasional	despaired	sulky
owl pellet	oblivious	conscience
plea	dismounted	

Section 4
(Chapters 9–11)

reminisced	bewildered	anxiously
conceded	scheme	temperature
fragrance	ventured	staunchly
entitled	feebly	pilfer
pandemonium	grateful	ebbed
agitated	huddled	rattle
ominously	squeaking	

Section 5
(Chapters 12–13)

frightened	glinting	sympathetic
aspirin	crucial	damage
gleaming	nuisance	responsible
difficulty	indignantly	opportunity
precious	exclaimed	composition
discovered	talons	imagination

8

Vocabulary Activity Ideas

You can help your students learn and retain the vocabulary in *The Mouse and the Motorcycle* by providing them with interesting vocabulary activities. It is always a good idea to have the words displayed somewhere in the class (a pocket chart, poster boards, or time line strip.) Here are a few ideas to try.

❑ Challenge your students to a **Vocabulary Bee**. This is similar to a spelling bee, but in addition to spelling each word correctly, the game participants must correctly define the words as well.

❑ **Around the World** — Make flashcards of each vocabulary word. The player holding the flashcards shows a card to two students. Whoever says the word first has to tell what the definition is. If that person can not tell the definition, then the other person has a chance. Whoever answers correctly pairs up with the next person in class. The game continues to see who can make it "around the world." (An option is to use the word in a sentence instead of telling the definition.)

❑ Ask your students to make their own **Crossword Puzzles** and **Word Search Puzzles** using the vocabulary from the story. Have them exchange papers and work the puzzles. When completed, the authors can correct the papers.

❑ **Grab Bag** — Write all the vocabulary words on small strips of paper and then place them in a jar, box, or bag. A representative from each team grabs a predetermined number of words. The team then writes a short story using these words.

❑ **Vocabulary Bingo** — Hand out blank bingo grids to students. Have them place one vocabulary word in each space on the grid. Students may place the words in any order on the sheet. Then, randomly choose and read the vocabulary definitions. A student wins by covering a row or column of words as the definitions are read.

❑ **Alpha-Omega** — Write the vocabulary words out on sentence strips. Each team comes to the front of the class where every member is handed a vocabulary strip. When the teacher says "Start!" the members must place the strips in alphabetical order. Each team will have a turn using different sets of words. The winning team will do their alphabetizing the quickest.

❑ **Word of the Day** — Students choose a vocabulary word and use it at least 10 times that day. The word can be used both orally or in a writing activity. Work with partners to help keep track.

❑ **Where in the World** — Ask your students to find the sentence in the book that contains the vocabulary word. Copy the sentence down; then, use the word in another sentence.

❑ **Vocabulary Charades** — In this game, vocabulary words are acted out.

❑ **Picture Dictionary** — Have the students work with partners or teams to create picture dictionaries using the vocabulary words.

You probably have many more ideas to add to this list. Try them all. See if experiencing vocabulary on a personal level increases your students' vocabulary interest and retention.

Quiz Time

1. On the back of this paper, write a one-paragraph summary of the major events in each chapter of this section. Then, complete the rest of the questions on this page.

2. What is the room number and name of the hotel where Keith is staying?

    _____

    _____

3. Describe Matt and his job at the Inn.

    _____

    _____

4. How does Mrs. Gridley feel about the Inn?

    _____

    _____

5. Describe the four different toys that Keith takes out of his suitcase.

    _____

    _____

    _____

6. Ralph experiences many feelings as he observes Keith unpacking. Name at least three of his emotions and tell why he feels them.

    _____

    _____

    _____

7. Why does Ralph's mother worry so much about him?

    _____

    _____

8. Describe the motorcycle.

    _____

    _____

9. Why does Ralph think that the motorcycle should run?

    _____

    _____

10. On the back of this paper, explain how Ralph ends up at the bottom of the wastebasket.

Motorcycle Madness

When Ralph first sets his eyes on the motorcycle and hears Keith make the pb-pb-b-b-b sound, his thoughts go to the speed of the open highway, the distance and danger, and the sensation of his whiskers blowing back in the wind. As Ralph examines the motorcycle more closely, he notices all the many details and parts that make up such a magnificent machine. He sees the chromium mufflers, the hand clutch and even the little license plate. Each motorcycle manufacturer (a company which makes things either by hand or machine) creates a special design for its bikes, but for the most part, all motorcycles are built the same and have similar parts. The picture below shows a basic motorcycle with some of the most important parts.

Parts Index

A. *Throttle:* controls the speed of the engine

B. *Handlebars:* steers the motorcycle

C. *Fork:* secures tires and has springs inside for a smoother ride

D. *Fuel Tank:* holds the fuel

E. *Brake:* slows down the wheels

F. *Exhaust:* takes away used gases from the engine

G. *Gearshift Lever:* changes the speed of the motorcycle

H. *Stand:* holds the bike up when not turned on

I. *Drive Chain:* moves by the gears to make the back wheel go around

J. *Engine:* provides power of the motorcycle

K. *Seat:* is used to sit upon

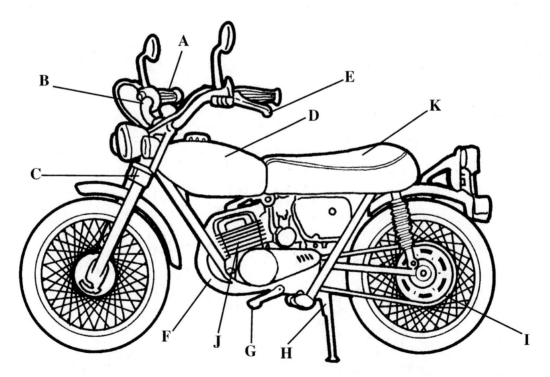

At each motorcycle manufacturer, there are designers whose jobs are to create pleasing and beautiful bike designs that are safe and functional. Also working with the designers are engineers. An engineer's job is to look at the designs and determine if they are possible to build. Once a design has been agreed upon, the engineers begin drawing blueprints. Blueprints are a set of instructions for the rest of the motorcycle plant to follow as the new motorcycle is built.

Motorcycle Madness *(cont.)*

Be a Designer

Pretend that you are a motorcycle designer. Your job is to design the ultimate motorcycle for the future. Your motorcycle will not even be introduced to the market for another 25 years, so you will really need to be imaginative and think ahead. What will your bike look like? Will it be the same size as today's motorcycles, bigger, or smaller? What kind of fuel will it run on? How fast will it go? What will its name be? Is it environmentally sound?

Draw a sketch of your design below. (Check for spelling with your teacher or study-buddy). Then, draw and color your motorcycle on a piece of construction paper for display. Be sure to label the parts.

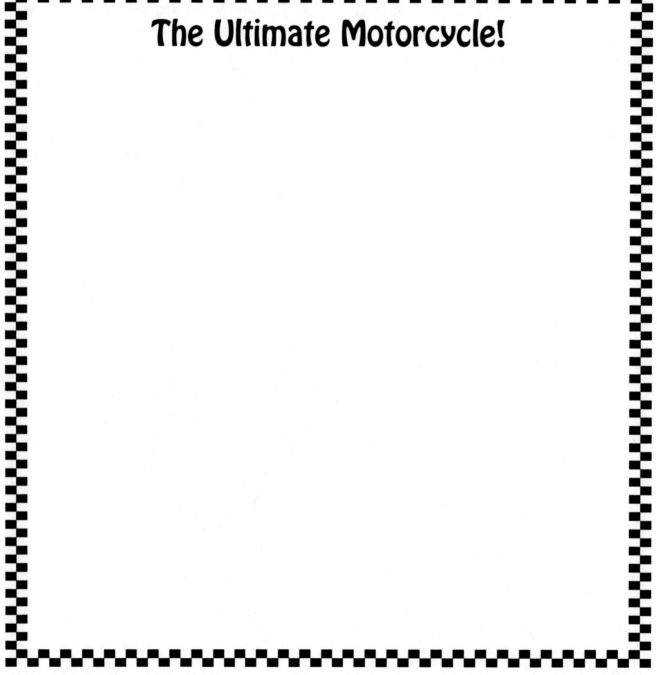

The Ultimate Motorcycle!

Measuring Up

Watching from his mousehole, Ralph observed Keith unpacking his toy cars and motorcycle. The cars — a sedan, a sports car, and an ambulance, were about six inches (15 cm) in length. The shiny, red motorcycle was half the length of the cars. How long would that be? Think of some other things that are about the same length as the toy cars (6 inches/15 cm).

When you want to find out the length of an object, the most common and accurate method of doing this is to use a ruler. A ruler is a **standard unit of measurement**. This means that all rulers are the same size and use the same numbers for measurement. A **nonstandard unit of measurement** is just the opposite. Just a couple of hundred years ago, a common nonstandard unit of measurement was the human hand. When farmers wanted to measure their horses, they used their hands and counted how many "hands high" a horse was. What problems would there be in this way of measuring?

Complete the following measuring activity with both nonstandard and standard units of measurement.

- **Nonstandard Unit of Measurement**

  You will need some string and scissors. Working with your partner, wrap the string once around your wrist and then cut off the piece of string that measures your wrist. This piece of string will be your "ruler" for measuring.

  As a class, choose 8 or 10 objects for everyone to measure with their "wrist rulers," for example, length of desk, new pencil, windowsill.

- **Share and Compare**

  When the whole class is finished measuring, share your findings. What do you notice? Are all the numbers the same? Why do you think the numbers are different?

- **Standard Unit of Measurement**

  You probably discovered that by using a nonstandard unit of measurement, the measurement numbers would not come out the same. Could this be a problem? Why or why not?

  Now, try measuring the same items. This time, use a standard unit of measurement — a ruler. Your teacher will instruct you as to whether you will measure in metric (millimeters, centimeters, meters) or U.S. Customary Units (inches, feet, yards). Record your findings in the chart on page 14.

- **Share and Compare**

  Once the class is finished measuring, share your findings again. As your teacher records the data, what do you notice that is different this time? Are the numbers the same? How do you and your partner's wrist rulers compare to standard measure? Do you think that it is important for people to use standard units of measure? Why or why not?

Measuring Up *(cont.)*

Use the data chart below with the activities on page 13.

Object	Wrist Ruler Measurment	Standard Measurment Using _____

Plot a Course

In *The Mouse and the Motorcycle*, the Gridley family planned a vacation traveling across part of the United States. Keith's family began their trip in their home state of Ohio and traveled over plains, deserts, and mountains before reaching the Mountain View Inn in the California foothills. Mr. and Mrs. Gridley wanted to show Keith as much of the United States as possible, so they planned a three-week trip.

Activity

Pretend that you are a travel agent and Keith's family has come to you for assistance in making their vacation plans. It is your job to plot out a route for them on a map of the United States. Highlight the attractions and points of interest that you feel they would enjoy seeing. (These could be cities, national parks, monuments, museums, natural wonders, etc.) Your teacher will provide you with some references, but be sure to visit the library or your local travel agent for some more information. Take into consideration the different time zones and travel time for the Gridley family. Propose a route that starts at some point in Ohio, travels to the Pacific Ocean, and then takes the family back home all in a three-week period.

Your finished product should include a map of the United States with a highlighted course of travel. Make your own map or use the one below. You should also include an itinerary, a traveler's guide outlining the schedule of events for a trip. The Gridley family itinerary should include dates, times of arrivals and departures, destinations, comments about the points of interest, and a log of miles traveled. Give your travel agency a name and include your own business card. Bon voyage!

Reading Response Journals

One great way to ensure that the reading of *The Mouse and the Motorcycle* touches each student in a personal way is to include the use of Reading Response Journals in your plans. In these journals, students can be encouraged to respond to the story in a number of ways. Here are a few ideas:

- Ask students to create a journal for *The Mouse and the Motorcycle*. Initially, have them assemble lined and unlined three-hole paper, brad-fastened or stapled, with a blank page for the journal's cover. As they read the story, they may draw a design on the cover that helps tell the story for them.

- Tell the students that the purpose of the journal is to record their thoughts, ideas, observations, and questions as they read *The Mouse and the Motorcycle.*

- Provide your students with, or ask them to suggest, topics from the story that would stimulate writing. Here are a few examples from the chapters in this section:

  — The Gridley family takes a three-week driving vacation so that they can see as much of the United States as possible. Would you like to go on a vacation like Keith's? Why or why not? What would be your ultimate vacation? Where would you go? With whom would you go? What adventures would you have?

  — When Keith begins unpacking his suitcase he takes out an apple, several small toy cars, and the motorcycle. When you go on a vacation or overnight trip somewhere, what are some of the things that you take with you? Why do you take them? What would you really like to take with you but for some reason are not able to?

  — Ralph climbs the telephone cord to get a closer look at the motorcycle and falls into the wastebasket. As he is falling, Ralph thinks of his Uncle Victor. Do you know someone who placed themselves in danger to get something they really wanted? What do you think of their actions?

- After reading each chapter, students can write one or more new things that they learned in the chapter. Ask students to draw their responses to certain events or characters in the story, using the unlined pages in their journals.

- Tell students that they may use their journals to record "diary-type" responses. Encourage students to bring their journal ideas to life. Ideas generated from their journal writing can be used to create plays, debates, stories, songs, and art displays.

- It is important to allow students time to write in their journals daily. Also, allow students the option to share their journal entries with the whole class at the end of writing time. Another strategy is to provide each child with a one-minute period in which to share his or her writing with members of the group. With this plan, all students are then participating in the oral portion of the language process.

Quiz Time

1. On the back of this paper, write a one-paragraph summary of the major events in each chapter of this section. Then, complete the rest of the questions on this page.

2. What happens to the motorcycle because of the fall?

   _____

   _____

3. What happens to Uncle Victor?

   _____

   _____

4. How does Ralph attempt to get out of the wastebasket?

   _____

   _____

5. Why does Ralph decide to finally talk with Keith?

   _____

   _____

6. Describe the tips that Keith gives to Ralph about riding the motorcycle.

   _____

   _____

7. When Ralph speeds past room 211, why does he become frightened?

   _____

   _____

8. Why do you think Ralph makes an offensive gesture to the terrier?

   _____

   _____

9. How does Ralph get back into Keith's room when the morning comes?

   _____

   _____

10. Ralph and Keith are not surprised that they can speak the same language to each other. Matt also can speak their language. On the back of this paper, explain why you think these three characters are able to communicate.

Racer Ralph

The thrill of racing and the excitement of adventure are what Ralph desires most in his mouse life. Now you can feel some of the same thrill that Ralph felt by building your very own Racer Ralph motorcycle. Follow the directions on this paper. (**Note to the teacher:** You may wish to enlarge the patterns on this page.)

Materials:

Cardboard or card stock paper, three paper fasteners (brads), a 7-inch (18 cm) balsa rod, colored crayons, pens or pencils, scissors, glue (or a glue gun)

Directions:

Color Ralph's body, Ralph's legs, the motorcycle, and the wheels. Cut out the patterns. Carefully trace the patterns onto the cardboard (except the legs). Cut out the cardboard pieces. Glue the body/motorcycle patterns to the body/motorcycle cardboard shapes. Using the paper fasteners, attach the wheels to the motorcycle points. Using the other paper fastener, attach the legs to Ralph's body. Allow Racer Ralph to dry for at least five minutes. Glue the tip of the balsa rod to the back of Ralph's body. Allow time to dry.

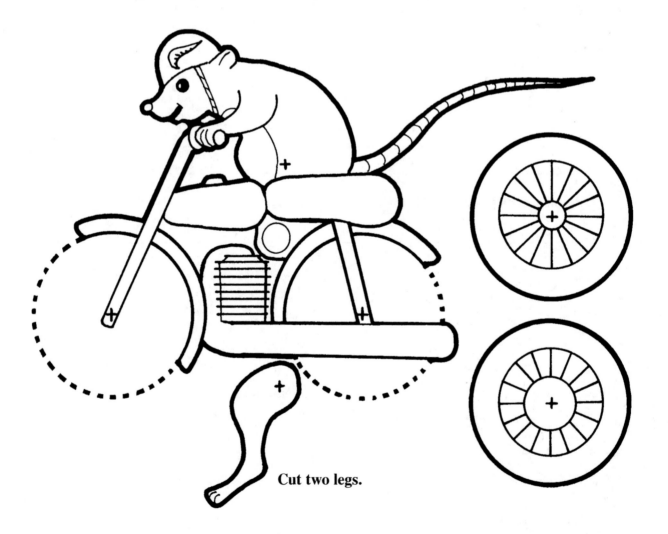

Cut two legs.

Workin' the Line

Long before Ralph ever laid eyes on the shiny, red motorcycle, a whole other world was at work. Back at the toy motorcycle factory, many, many hands were busily working to put together the masterpiece that Keith and Ralph called a motorcycle. While putting together a toy motorcycle is indeed an involved task, assembling an actual life-sized motorcycle is a very elaborate process. The creation of a motorcycle requires several different people with many unique skills to piece together the final product. Harley-Davidson is the only American manufacturer of motorcycles. No one person builds an entire engine or an entire bike at Harley-Davidson. Instead, many people work along an assembly line, with each person responsible for only one or two steps in the total assembly. An assembly line is a grouping of machines, equipment, and workers so that work passes from station to station in a direct line until the product is assembled. Thousands of worker hours go into a Harley-Davidson motorcycle's design and structure.

Today you will be working with a group and participating in an actual assembly line. Working on an assembly line is a lot like working in groups. Instead of sitting in a circle or at a cluster of desks, however, you will be standing in a line.

The Super, Stupendous, and Scrumptious Sandwich Factory

Your class will be divided into groups of six members each. Each group will become an assembly line. The factory job for today is to produce large quantities of peanut butter and jelly sandwiches. Each worker on the assembly line is very important. If just one person does not do his or her job, then the end product will not be finished. Let's all work together!

The line members' responsibilities are as follows:

1. initial bread passer
2. peanut-butter scooper and knife prep
3. peanut-butter spreader
4. jelly scooper and knife prep
5. jelly spreader
6. sandwich combiner and stacker

Determine which worker will be in charge of what job and begin the assembly line. Just for fun, your teacher will time you, and the teams can compare their processes. One important thing to remember in assembly line work — speed is important, but quality is more important.

A Flash of History

Both Ralph and Keith have great respect for motorcycles and think that they are extremely exciting and fun. It was through their love of motorcycles that their friendship began. The beginning of motorcycles, however, started long before Keith and Ralph became good friends. Read about the different kinds of motorcycles that have been created and see how they have changed over time.

- **A German man named Karl von Drais invented a two-wheeled machine called a *Hobby Horse* in sketches in 1817.**
- **In 1861 a Frenchman named Pierre Michaux put pedals on both sides of the front wheel of the *Hobby Horse* and called his invention the *Velocipede*.**
- **In 1868 L.G. Perreaux, also from France, fitted a steam engine to the *Velocipede* and created the *Velo a Vapeur*.**
- **In 1876 a German engineer named Gottlieb Daimler, used a small gasoline tank for fuel and attached this engine to a bicycle. He called his invention the *Einspur*, and it became a huge success.**
- **In 1894 two Germans, Hildebrand and Wolfmuller, began the mass manufacturing of the *Motorrad*.**
- **By 1904 the motorcycle craze soon caught on in the United States and was led by two Americans, William Harley and Arthur Davidson. *Harley-Davidson* motorcycles became famous because they were strong and seldom broke down.**

(Information found in *Looking at Motorcycles*, Cliff Lines, Bookwright Press, 1985, and *Motorcycle: The Making of a Harley-Davidson*, William Jaspersohm, Little, Brown and Company, 1984)

As you can see, one great idea was changed and improved over time. What began as the two-wheeled, saddled machine powered by the speed of the rider's feet soon grew to the exciting, high-powered and speed-generating engine that it is today. When Ralph first sat upon that shiny, red motorcycle, admiring the sparkling chrome and dreaming of exhilarating speed, did he wonder about the history of a motorcycle? Whether he did or did not, it is plain to see that over the course of time, Ralph was not the only creature craving the thrill of speed.

Activity:

Using a piece of construction paper and the information above, make a time line. Show the date, the name of the motorcycle, and the inventor.

The DMV and You

Ralph is on his way to speed and adventure now. With Keith's motorcycle, he is in store for some terrific times. But if he is not careful, he could be in store for some dangerous times, as well. Operating any kind of machinery can be hazardous unless the driver uses caution and practices safety. Every state has a Department of Motor Vehicles (DMV). This is a public service agency that gives out permits and licenses to people who want to drive a vehicle. The DMV hopes that by educating drivers on the laws and testing people on their driving abilities, it will be able to help cut down the number of traffic accidents. To legally drive a car, truck, bus, or motorcycle, a person needs to pass a test to get a driver's license. The laws for getting a motorcycle operator license are different in each state. Ralph's state was California. In some states a person has to be only 14 years old to legally drive a motorcycle, and in other states, a driver must be 21.

Directions:

Your teacher will be giving you a motorcycle driver supplement handbook from your local DMV. It is a fairly long book with a lot of information, so your job today will be to skim the book and look for certain facts. With your partner, browse through the handbook and answer the questions below. By the time you are through discovering some motorcycle information, you will have become quite an expert.

1. List two suggestions that the DMV gives in choosing a helmet.

2. What kind of clothing is good to wear when riding a motorcycle?

3. Motorcycles have two sets of brakes. Which is the more powerful of the two?

4. What are the three signals that all vehicles use for turning and stopping? (left turn, right turn, slow or stop)

5. What is a "tailgater"?

6. Name three examples of dangerous surfaces for a motorcycle.

7. What is some advice for the motorcycle rider who travels at night?

8. In order to carry a passenger on a motorcycle, what two things must the bike have?

9. Some motorcycle riders like to ride in groups. The best way to do this is in a staggered formation. How many seconds should the riders be apart?

10. Studies show that about 45% of all riders killed in motorcycle crashes have been drinking alcohol. What is the legal limit of blood alcohol concentration (BAC) for your state?

Bonus: Write a letter to Ralph and explain to him some of the rules for riding a motorcycle in your state. Give him some safety and driving tips, too.

Quiz Time

1. On the back of this page, write a one-paragraph summary of the major events in each chapter of this section. Then, complete the rest of the questions on this page.

2. Why does Ralph think that it must be terrible to go through life without fur?

   _____

   _____

3. What are Ralph and his family accustomed to eating? What is their first room-service treat?

   _____

   _____

4. What promise does Ralph make to Keith?

   _____

   _____

5. Describe how Ralph escapes the vacuum's suction.

   _____

   _____

6. What is the important experiment that Ralph wants to conduct?

   _____

   _____

7. What choice does Ralph make about how to get out of the linen pile?

   _____

   _____

8. Ralph feels even worse about the motorcycle when Keith gives him a present. What is the gift?

   _____

   _____

9. What is it that Keith says to Ralph that could not have hurt him more?

   _____

   _____

10. Even more than feeling angry with Ralph, Keith is disappointed in him. On the back of this paper, write about a time that someone you cared a lot about felt disappointed in you. How did you feel?

Crash Helmet

The very first time that Ralph rides the motorcycle, he has an accident. Fortunately for Ralph, he is not seriously hurt. Being safe on a motorcycle is extremely important. Some states have laws that require all motorcycle riders to wear helmets. Later on in the story, Keith designs and makes a special crash helmet for Ralph. The helmet he creates for Ralph is made out of a Ping-Pong ball with thistledown for padding.

Helmets for human bikers, however, are much more sturdy. In order for a helmet to pass the Department of Transportation's test for safety, it must weigh at least three pounds. The helmet is generally made from a fiberglass material or a special carbon fiber. The inside padding consists of a hardened Styrofoam. Just one inch (5 cm) of Styrofoam padding is enough to save a bruise to the brain in an accident. This is sometimes the difference between life and death. All smart motorcycle riders wear helmets.

Here is an opportunity for you to make a crash helmet like the one Keith made.

Materials:

- one half of one Ping-Pong ball
- rubber band
- cotton ball
- glue stick (or a glue gun)
- (permanent ink markers, fine point)

Directions:

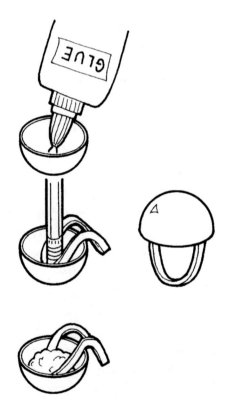

1. If you are using a glue gun, be sure to have an adult assist you.
2. Place a dab of glue into the center of the inside of the Ping-Pong half.
3. Carefully place one side of the rubber band into the glue. (Use a pencil tip to help push down the rubber band.)
4. When the rubber band is secure, drop a dab of glue onto the rubber band (the part inside the Ping-Pong ball half).
5. Place the cotton onto the glue.
6. Let it sit for five minutes to dry.
7. When your crash helmet is dry, use permanent ink markers to decorate your helmet. Be sure to allow time for your artwork to dry; otherwise, it is easy to smudge.

For extra fun, use a shoe box to make a diorama of a motorcycle store. You could use your helmet as one of the display items.

Designing Your School Menu

When it comes to eating, Ralph and his family eat basically whatever they can get their paws on. So when Keith asks Ralph what he would like to eat, Ralph is astounded. This is the first time in his little mouse life that anyone had asked him what he would like to eat. He did not realize that he had a choice. Not only does he get to choose the meal, but Keith will bring it up to the room just like room service.

Just about every hotel all around the world offers some sort of room service. Room service means that a hotel guest may order a meal or snack from the hotel kitchen and have the meal brought to their room. Most hotels offer room service for breakfast, lunch, and dinner. Some hotels even offer room service 24 hours a day. If a guest gets the "midnight munchies," he or she could order a pizza or some chips and dip.

Ralph chooses a peanut butter and jelly sandwich for his first room service meal. The next meal from room service is a chocolate chip cookie and blueberry muffin. This is such a treat that Ralph's family has a reunion.

Since most children have not stayed in hotels before, much less ordered room service, your team will design a school lunch menu. Here is your chance to create and select a scrumptious menu. With your team members, design a school breakfast and lunch menu for the whole week, which will include the following: breakfast, lunch, snacks, prices, hours of operation, and the name of the cafeteria.

A good menu will fully describe each meal to help the students decide what they want to order. Some menus provide pictures with their descriptions. A menu can be on one piece of paper. Many menus are arranged so that they can be folded.

Directions

1. Discuss with your team members how the menu will be planned. Will it be a fold-out or a one page menu? Will it include pictures? How many choices for each meal? Will it be a 24-hour operation or open just certain hours? Determine the price ranges.

2. Next, determine the job(s) for each team member. Who will be in charge of the cover design? Will each person be in charge of a meal and all the selections? Who will do the drawings? Will each member draw for him/herself? How will all the pieces of the menu be put together? What other questions should your team ask in order to create a superb menu?

3. Begin designing and assembling the menu. Your teacher will provide your team with the necessary paper. Make it colorful and eye catching. Share your menus with the class when you are finished. Display all the class menus on a special bulletin board.

Famous Mice . . . Mouse Von Trapp?

After being trapped in the wastebasket, learning to ride the motorcycle, escaping a barking dog, and seeking adventure, Ralph is earning himself quite a reputation. No doubt by the end of *The Mouse and the Motorcycle*, Ralph will become quite a famous mouse. (At least at the Mountain View Inn!) There are many famous and popular mice throughout the world.

You can find famous mice in fairy tales, fables, and nursery rhymes. Remember the three blind mice? Or the mouse that ran up the grandfather clock? What about the mice in the Cinderella tale who were turned into coachmen? There is the fable of the city mouse and the country mouse. And you probably have heard of the kind mouse who saved the lion by pulling a thorn from his paw. Probably the most famous of all, though, was a mouse "born" in 1928, Mickey Mouse. Mickey's creator, Walt Disney, said that "Mickey represents the clever, tiny mouse hunted by everybody."

Mice have been on this planet for more than 8,000 years. Mice belong to a group of similar animals called rodents. Some examples of rodents are rats, hamsters, gerbils, and guinea pigs. Nearly one-half of all the known mammals in the world are rodents. More than 4,000 years ago, many ancient civilizations revered mice and considered them good luck from their gods. The people of Crete even built a temple where they fed and worshipped mice.

Virtually all wild mice are a brown or gray color, but the most popular color for pet mice is white with pink eyes. The smallest mouse in the world is the African dwarf mouse which is not more than 2 inches (5 cm) and weighs less than 1/5 of an ounce (5.6 g)! The largest mouse, on the other hand, is from South America. It is called a capybara, or "water pig," and grows to more than 48 inches (1.2 meters) and weighs over 200 pounds (90 kg). Imagine this mouse on a motorcycle! Even though many people consider mice to be cute and charming, wild mice are very destructive. They destroy crops, carry diseases, and chew human belongings. For these reasons, humans are continually trying to find ways to control the mouse population. Some mice, however, will always be safe from hunters. These mice are the "famous mice."

(Disney quote taken from *Mice, a Complete Pet Owner's Manual*, Bielfeld, 1985)

The Before and After Story

For this activity you will need to choose the story of a famous mouse. Use one that has already been mentioned or go to the library and pick a different mouse tale or rhyme. Read the story again. As you read, ask yourself these following questions:

1. What was this mouse doing before the story started?
2. Did this mouse have a family? Brothers and sisters? Friends?
3. Where did the mouse live?
4. Did this mouse go to school? Work? Was this mouse happy?
5. What happened to the mouse after the story ended?
6. Did the mouse change his/her life in any way?
7. Where did the mouse end up 10 years later?
8. Did the mouse learn anything after the experience in the story?

Famous Mice . . .
Mouse Von Trapp? *(cont.)*

Your job is to make a complete version of this little mouse's life. All stories should have a beginning, middle, and end. Pretend that the story you chose is the "middle" and you are to design the beginning and end. Use the lines below to plan the begining and end of your story. Write "before-the-story" and "after-the-story" editions for this famous mouse on separate paper. Be as creative as humanly possible. Provide lots of details; make it funny and silly or realistic and sad, if you wish. Bring this popular mouse to life. When you are finished writing the "before/after ideas," share the stories with your friends.

Before-the-Story Ideas

_____

_____

_____

_____

_____

_____

After-the-Story Ideas

_____

_____

_____

_____

_____

_____

It's All in the Family

Ralph comes from a big family with many brothers and sisters. He also has several of his relatives living nearby at the Mountain View Inn. His Aunt Sissy lives in the bridal suite, his Uncle Lester lives in the housekeeper's office, and Aunt Dorothy lives close by. Ralph can remember some of his older relatives that used to live at the Inn, like Uncle Victor. Do you come from a big family? Do your relatives live nearby, or do you have to travel a long distance to visit with them? Where is your family originally from?

The Family Tree

Getting to know your family's history can be fun and informative. Even though your ancestors may have died many years ago, it is interesting to learn about the stories of their lives. Someday, your great-great grandchildren will be wondering about you. With the help of your parents or grandparents, complete this family tree to the best of your ability. As you complete your family tree, ask your parents/grandparents if they remember any stories about your ancestors.

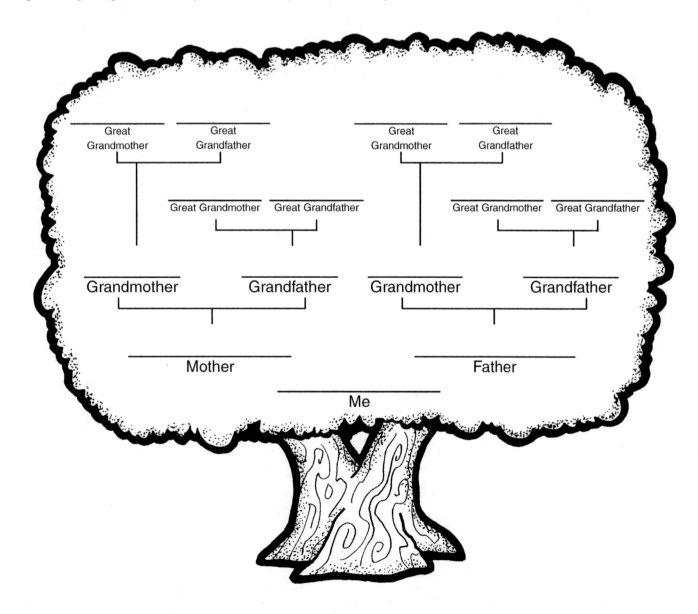

It's All in the Family *(cont.)*

The Ralph Mouse Family Reunion and Your Family Reunion

When Ralph's family gets together for a reunion, there is an abundance of food and activity. The little brothers and sisters finish their dinner and race around the house. Cousins fight over the blueberries. Overweight uncles ask for second helpings, and the adults have to raise their voices in order to be heard over the racket the children make. Are your family reunions anything like Ralph's? How are they different? Think about the similarities and differences between Ralph's family and your family and then complete the Venn diagram below.

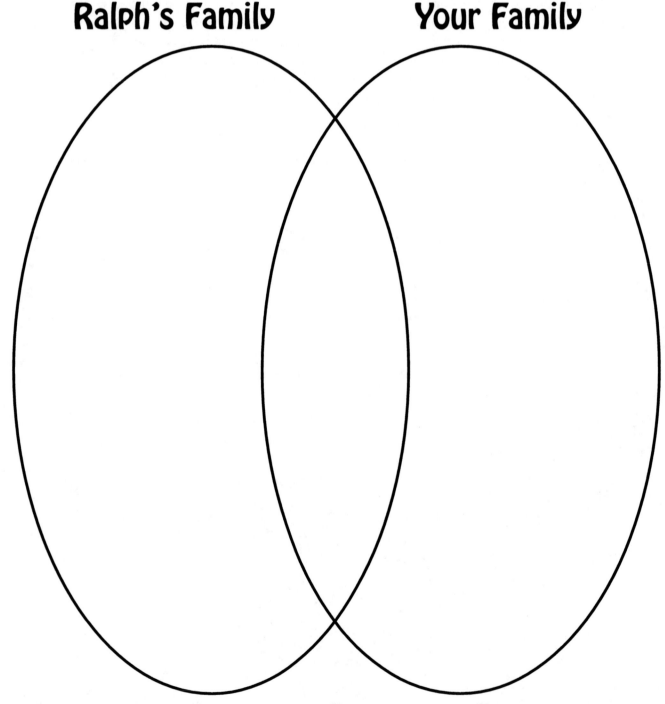

Ralph's Family   **Your Family**

Quiz Time

1. On the back of this page, write a one-paragraph summary of the major events in each chapter of this section. Then, complete the rest of the questions on this page.

2. Where does Ralph go the night he tells Keith about the motorcycle, and why does he go there?

   _____

   _____

3. Why does Keith decide not to be so angry with Ralph? (Use examples.)

   _____

   _____

4. Describe the pandemonium that Ralph discovers back in the mousehole. Why is everybody so upset?

   _____

   _____

5. What change comes over Ralph as the family panics about the war on mice?

   _____

   _____

6. What happens to Keith, and what is needed to help him?

   _____

   _____

7. Why does Ralph decide to risk his life to help Keith?

   _____

   _____

8. What occupations do Betty and Mary Lou have? How do you know?

   _____

   _____

9. What does Mary Lou say about Ralph that hurts his feelings?

   _____

   _____

10. Think about a time that you felt very strongly about helping someone. Maybe you wanted to help your sister or brother, a friend, or a stranger in need. Using the back of this paper, tell about this time. Be sure to explain why you felt so strongly.

Dress the Part

Not only does Keith let Ralph use his motorcycle and forgive him when Ralph loses it, but he also makes a special crash helmet to keep Ralph safe when he rides. A helmet is a very important accessory to a motorcycle rider, probably the most important. There are many different accessories that bikers have and like to use while enjoying their motorcycles. Some riders have special jackets with neat designs on the back. Most jackets are made from leather, as this is a durable fabric which helps to protect a rider in case of an accident. If a rider is a member of a motorcycle club, there may be club T-shirts to wear. Some motorcycles even have little antenna flags flying in the wind as they ride. Each rider is an individual, and the kinds of accessories that he/she chooses are a way to express this individuality. Pretend that you own a motorcycle shop that specializes in rider apparel and accessories.

Activity

Ralph decides that he needs more than a helmet. He comes to your store to choose some new accessories. In the squares, design some accessories (a jacket, helmet, T-shirt, boots, decal, gloves, etc.) that you think Ralph would enjoy. Be sure to give your motorcycle shop a name.

Shop Name _____

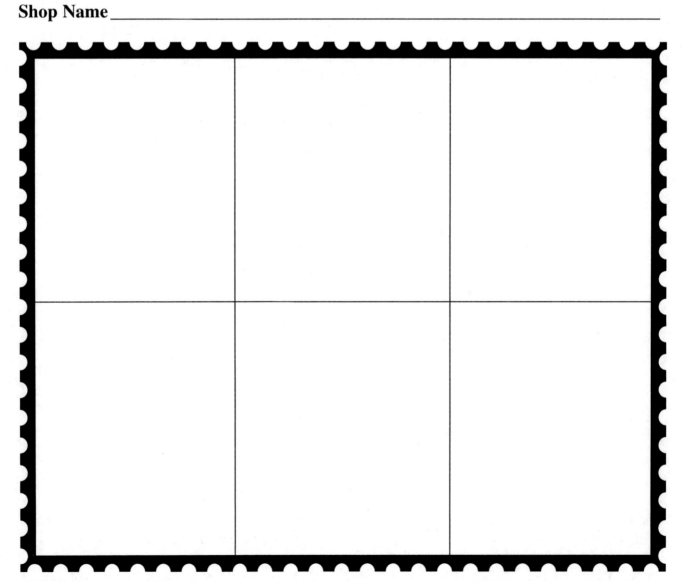

Laughable Limericks

Poetry is an enjoyable way to tell a story or convey ideas, thoughts, and feelings. Poetry can be serious, sad, joyful, or humorous. *The Mouse and the Motorcycle* is a story about adventures, friendship, and some silly times.

What is a limerick?

A limerick is a rhyming, five-line humorous poem. The key element in a limerick is humor.

Limericks often begin with "There once was a _____named_____.

Most limericks are five lines long and follow these rules:

- Lines 1, 2, and 5 rhyme and have eight to ten syllables.

- Lines 3 and 4 rhyme and have five to seven syllables.

Read the following limerick about Grace, the chocolate lover.

There once was a young girl named Grace,

Who wore chocolate all over her face.

When asked why that's so,

She replied, "Don't you know?

I can't find a towel anyplace!"

Think about the humorous events in *The Mouse and the Motorcycle*. On the lines below, write a limerick about Ralph and Keith and the antics they shared. If you wish, you may work with a partner. Share your poem with the class.

_____

_____

_____

_____

_____

_____

_____

Acids, Neutrals, and Covering Your Bases

Ralph courageously sets off to find an aspirin for Keith who is sick with a high fever. Keith is smart to wait until the morning to ask his parents if it is okay to take the aspirin since he knows it is a drug. Aspirin is one of the most commonly used drugs in the world. Aspirin is a basically safe drug when taken at the recommended dosage levels. However, it may irritate some people's stomachs and cause stomach bleeding in some cases. This is because aspirin is an acid substance. Chemists divide substances into different groups. These three groups are called acids, bases, and neutrals. A base is the opposite of an acid. Bases have a bitter taste and often feel slippery or soapy. Baking soda is a type of base. A neutral substance is one that does not seem to be an acid or a base. Water is an example of a neutral substance. When chemists and scientists do experiments with unknown substances, one of the first things they do is try to determine if the "mystery" substance is an acid, base, or neutral. Today you will be conducting the same kind of experiment. You will be given a variety of powders and liquids, and your job will be to discover what group each substance fits into — acids, bases, or neutrals. Like all successful scientists, at the end of your experiment you will write a brief summary of what you observed and discovered.

Materials and Equipment

- juice from red cabbage (indicator)
- water source
- clear containers such as baby-food jars
- 3 large glass jars
- ammonia (Adult supervision is required.)
- plastic sandwich bags
- cream of tartar
- hammer or kitchen meat pounder
- vitamin C tablets
- plastic stirrers
- aspirin tablets
- eye droppers
- apple juice
- masking tape
- orange juice
- tea (brewed from bags)
- a solution of scouring powder
- coffee
- baking soda
- soda pop
- Alka-Seltzer (or another commercial antacid)
- (You may want to add to this list as you begin to wonder what substances are acids, bases, and neutrals.)

Directions:

Many of the substances you will be working with today are dangerous to swallow. Please use common sense and good safety skills while conducting this experiment. Your teacher will give you instructions as you work on this activity.

Use the cabbage juice as the neutral substance. Pour the cabbage juice into several jars. Slowly add one of the other substances to a jar using an eye dropper. Notice a change in the cabbage juice color. (Red means an acid, blue means a base, and no change in color means the substance is neutral.) Test the substances that you are provided with. Observe how many drops of each substance are needed to change the indicator color. Some of the substances are in a solid form (aspirin, vitamin C, antacid, etc.). Place solids in a plastic bag and crush them into a powder using a hammer or meat pounder. Then, mix the powder with water. Complete your own data chart by recording your color change results. Write examples of data from your chart and draw conclusions based on your results.

The Pet Shop

Have you ever had a mouse, rat, or hamster for a pet? Rodents can make great pets and provide a lot of pleasure to their owners. Would you enjoy having Ralph for a pet mouse? Speaking the same language with your pet would be neat. It would be pretty hard to imagine Ralph wanting to live in a cage and become somebody's pet, even if that somebody was Keith.

Activity

If you have ever had a pet, you know there are many responsibilities involved. Pets need to be cared for, fed, cleaned, exercised, and loved on a regular basis. Having a pet is very much like being a parent. For this activity, you will pretend to buy a pet mouse. Your job is to research and purchase all the necessary equipment, food, toys, and whatever else is needed to make your mouse happy and healthy. You will be given a budget of $50.00, so be sure to stay in that budget. After you have set up your pet mouse's home, write a quick reference guide about your new mouse. Maybe you could call this helpful book "Important Mice Advice." This will be a mini-book telling anyone who reads it important tips on handling and caring for mice.

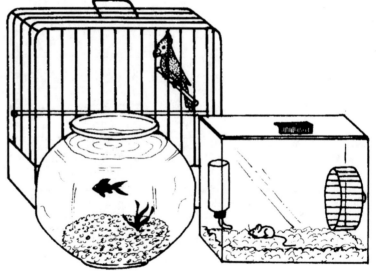

A good way to find information on mouse care is to visit a local pet store. If you and a friend decide to do this, be sure to call the owner or manager first to make an appointment. By doing this, you will be assured of reserving some special time with the owner, as well as respecting his/her busy schedule. Another source for you to use is the library. There are many, many books about mice and ideas on how to keep one as a pet.

Below is a partial listing of some significant facts for pet mouse care.

- A standard ten-gallon glass aquarium makes a nice home for mice. Small aquariums are inexpensive and easy to keep clean.
- The foods most commonly eaten by mice are seeds, lettuce, and carrots. Unlike Ralph, mice should not be fed human food.
- Mice are very social creatures and live in colonies in the wild. It is best to have two mice for their social happiness and health. A good combination is two females. Two males will constantly fight. A female and male is also a good combination, but you may end up with more mice than you bargained for.
- Buying the mouse is the last step. Always buy your mouse from a clean pet store that takes good care of its animals. Choose animals that are lively, slender, and alert. Their eyes should be wide open. Do not buy a mouse that wheezes or coughs.

For your project, keep a tally of your "expenses" and try to stay within your budget. Give your pretend new pet mouse a name and draw an illustration of your pet in its new home. For your "Mice Advice" book, jot down any ideas or suggestions that you have found.

Quiz Time

1. On the back of this page, write a one-paragraph summary of the major events in each chapter of this section. Then, complete the rest of the questions on this page.

2. Where does Ralph finally find an aspirin?

_____

_____

3. Where does Ralph hide the aspirin while he puts his plan into action?

_____

_____

4. What sound does the ambulance make?

_____

_____

5. Explain Ralph's plan for taking the aspirin up to Keith's room.

_____

_____

6. How do Keith's parents explain the aspirin ending up on the table?

_____

_____

7. What privilege does Ralph earn from his mother after showing how responsible he has become?

_____

_____

8. What is the secret that Keith learns about growing up?

_____

_____

9. Why does Keith give Ralph the motorcycle to keep for his own?

_____

_____

10. What lessons about growing up do both Ralph and Keith learn?

_____

_____

_____

_____

_____

Ralph's Adventure Map

When Ralph realizes that Keith is sick, not from eating too many peanuts or too much hiking but really and truly sick, he becomes worried. He thinks about how Keith has saved him from the terrible fate in the wastebasket. He thinks about the boy who has fed his family, who has trusted him with his motorcycle, and how Keith has even forgiven him when he has lost that. Ralph is determined to help. Go back and read about the path that Ralph takes in order to find an aspirin. Then, draw a map showing the route that he takes. Be sure to make a legend and include landmarks of the different places where he stops.

Readers' Theater

There was never a dull moment in *The Mouse and the Motorcycle*. Ralph is always trying to stay out of trouble but find adventure at the same time. Keith is trying not to grow up too fast. Ralph's relatives are often involved in some sort of activity, and both Keith and Ralph's mothers are worried about their sons.

In groups of two to five people, choose an event from the story that the group would enjoy acting out. Another option is to create a scenario which is based on an event, which happened in *The Mouse and the Motorcycle*. Your team will write a script retelling the event and each student will perform in the mini-play. Give your characters emotion and life. Feel free to add your own interpretation of each character. Here are some ideas for events in the story which could be written about and performed:

- the night that Keith found Ralph in the metal wastebasket
- the first time Ralph rode the motorcycle down the hallway
- Ralph's family receiving room service the first time
- Ralph almost getting sucked up by the vacuum cleaner and then chewing his way out of the linen
- Ralph telling Keith that he lost the motorcycle
- the family reunion
- the night that Ralph found the aspirin

Be sure that every group member has an opportunity to write part of the script. When the script is finished, practice going over it together and then perform it for the rest of the class, for parents, or for other classes. An invitation is provided below.

You are invited to our Readers' Theater presentations based on

The Mouse and the Motorcycle

When _____

Where _____

Please Join Us!

_____

Dem Bones

Ralph and his family are always worried about the owls that live just outside the Mountain View Inn. The owl is a natural predator of mice, small birds, and other small animals. Most animals have a natural predator. A predator is an enemy of another animal because it will eat the other animal for food. All plants and animals (including humans) are part of a complex natural system called the **food chain**. All living creatures require food to live. Some creatures eat only plants (like cows, mice, most whales, and rabbits), while other creatures will eat both plants and other animals (owls, snakes, lions, and human beings). A *food chain* is a string of events involving the consumption and production of food.

Activity

Today you have an opportunity to use your scientific mind and conduct a dissection experiment on owl pellets. *Dissection* means cutting and dividing something into several parts in order to analyze and understand it. By dissecting the contents of an owl's pellet, you will be able to determine what that owl's diet was for a period of time. You will also classify the pellet contents and try to "piece" the bones together in order to determine what animal skeletons are found.

Materials and Equipment

- owl pellet for each student (or partners)
- scissors
- two toothpicks per pellet
- newspaper
- paper towel
- pen or pencil for observations

Dissection — The pellet is very dry and will come apart easily, so handle it with care.

1. Spread the newspaper out on your desk or table.

2. Using a toothpick, carefully poke a hole in one end of the pellet.

3. Insert the tip of the scissors into the hole and begin cutting across the top of the pellet. Do not cut too deeply. Cut as close to the surface as possible.

4. Using your fingers and toothpicks, pull the pellet open from the center.

5. Gently begin picking apart the layers of the pellet.

6. As you come across a bone or questionable remain, remove it and place it on your paper towel. Some bones are more brittle than others, so handle them gently.

7. Complete the dissection until the entire pellet has been picked apart and all the remains have been removed.

Observe the bones that you have collected. Based on the mouse skeletal pictures you may have seen, do any of them look familiar? Begin picking out what appear to be backbones, leg and wing bones, and skulls. Design your own system of classifying the bone collection that you have. When the class is finished dissecting and classifying their information, your teacher will record the total bone types found on a class chart.

Be Our Guest

By the end of the story, Ralph becomes very confident riding the motorcycle. With Keith's help and some practice, he becomes a safe and competent rider. After reading *The Mouse and the Motorcycle,* as well as doing some of the chapter activities, you, too, probably know a little bit more about motorcycles. Another excellent way to learn more about a topic is to ask an expert.

There are plenty of motorcycle experts in the world. There are the professional motorcycle racers, the designers and engineers, the assembly-line workers in motorcycle factories, the helmet and accessory makers, the safety testers, and even the state highway patrol officers who often ride motorcycles. Did you know that there is probably a motorcycle expert right in your home town? The owner or employee of the local motorcycle shop is very knowledgeable when it comes to motorcycles. Invite this person to come and visit your class. Perhaps this expert will ride a motorcycle to your class so that you can get a closeup look.

Preparing for the Guest Speaker

- Elect a class spokesperson to briefly summarize *The Mouse and the Motorcycle.* Be sure to include the part about Ralph falling off the table and almost getting sucked up by the vacuum.

- Make a list of questions to ask the motorcycle expert. Some sample questions might include:

  - What are some important safety tips?
  - What kind of gas mileage does the motorcycle get?
  - How did you learn to ride a motorcycle?
  - What is the most popular motorcycle today?

Guest Speaker Tips

People who come in to visit your class are usually taking time away from their busy schedules to talk with you. It is important to be respectful of their time. One way that you can help them is by being prepared with some questions. Another way to respect their time is to ask questions, not tell stories. But if the speaker does ask the class to share some experiences, then by all means do!

Dear Mr. Turner,

We would like to thank you for taking the time out of your busy day to visit us.

Our class learned a lot about motorcycles and how they work.

Yours truly,
Mr. Robyn's Class

Thanks a Million

After your guest speaker has left, write him/her a special thank-you card. Include some of your original artwork, like a picture of the expert on a motorcycle, or maybe even a drawing of Ralph riding along beside the speaker. Your teacher will mail these letters for you.

Book Report Ideas

There are so many different ways to do a book report. After you finish reading *The Mouse and the Motorcycle*, choose one of the following methods of reporting that interests you. If you have an idea of your own, ask your teacher if you may do that instead. Have fun and be creative!

- **Dress 'n' Guess**

  Come to class dressed as one of the characters. Tell the class your version of the story from that character's perspective. Act like that character and answer any questions the class may have about you and your life.

- **Pen Pal**

  Write a letter to one of the characters in *The Mouse and the Motorcycle*. Tell him/her how your life is like and unlike his/hers. Ask that character questions and offer your opinions about some of the situations in the story. Then, write a letter back to yourself, pretending to be that character.

- **Talk-Show Host**

  Pretend that you are a television talk-show host and will be interviewing a character from *The Mouse and the Motorcycle*. Compose a list of questions that your viewers would be interested in. Ask one of your friends to be the character and then conduct a "live taping" of your show or produce a video.

- **Movie Marquee**

  The Mouse and the Motorcycle is about to become a major movie, and you have been chosen to design the promotional poster. Include the title, author of the book, a listing of the major characters in the book and the actors and actresses who will play them, and a short paragraph summarizing the story.

- **Mobile Magic**

  Create and assemble an exciting and colorful mobile to display in your classroom. Using a coat hanger, string, or fishing wire and heavy paper, show the plot, setting, and characters of *The Mouse and the Motorcycle*. Start by placing the setting at the top level, the characters at the middle level, and the plot development at the bottom level.

- **Mystery Box Game**

  Cover a shoe box with construction paper and color large question marks all over the box. On one side of the box, write the title of the book. Fill your box with five objects that are related to *The Mouse and the Motorcycle*. (Examples could be an aspirin, a toy motorcycle, or car.) Allow the class time to ask "yes" or "no" questions about the objects. When someone correctly guesses the object, he/she will need to explain how the object relates to the story.

- **Patchwork Quilt**

  Use a piece of 18" x 26"(45 cm x 65 cm) tagboard and six 8" x 8"(20 cm x 20 cm) squares of paper. Glue the squares on the tagboard and simulate "stitching" around each piece using a crayon or marker. Then, each of the squares will tell specific information about *The Mouse and the Motorcycle*. One square should state the title and author, and the other squares should tell about the characters, plot, and settings.

Book Buddy Brainstorm

In Beverly Cleary's book, *The Mouse and the Motorcycle*, she chose an animal and an unlikely contraption to go together. It is not often that when we think of mice we think of mice riding motorcycles! This is a sign of a good author. A successful writer will use his/her imagination and sometimes write about things that are out of the ordinary. Not only does this get the reader's attention, but this strategy of storytelling makes the book very interesting and entertaining.

Making a Book Buddy

For this activity you will use the same kind of writing idea that Beverly Cleary did. Instead of writing a whole book, however, you will make a Book Buddy. A Book Buddy is like making the skeleton of the book. This is a place to keep your ideas, draw pictures, try out a few adventure story lines, and create several different endings instead of just one. You can always go back and write the book later, but for now just have some fun brainstorming. To begin your brainstorm, write in 10 different kinds of animals on the lines below. (This list could include insects, birds, reptiles, mammals, and fish, if you like.)

1. _____
2. _____
3. _____
4. _____
5. _____
6. _____
7. _____
8. _____
9. _____
10. _____

For your second list, think up some "things" that begin with the same letters of the animal names. Create at least two "things" for each animal. For example:

Animal: Elephant   **Thing: 1. eggbeater 2. elevator**

Review the list and decide which animal and matching "thing" you will use for your activity. As soon as you have made your choice, write it here:

The _____**and the** _____.

Book Buddy Cover

Now, draw the cover for your book. Be sure to include the title, the author's name (could be you, a friend, some imaginary name, or even Beverly Cleary), and an eye-catching picture. Look at the cover of *The Mouse and the Motorcycle* and other books to get some ideas.

Book Buddy Brainstorm *(cont.)*

Colorful Characters

In order to make your story more interesting, add a few colorful characters. Think about your main character and what his interests are. Now, think of a few other characters who would add some action and excitement to the book. These characters could be friends, family members, older, younger, or from different animal groups. Remember that all good stories have a problem and then a solution, so maybe a situation with one of your characters could be part of the problem. On the chart below, use a few words to describe each character. Tell its name, what kind of animal it is (humans included!), what its personality is like, and how this character relates to the main character of your story.

Character Name	Animal Group	Personality Traits	Relating

Book Buddy Brainstorm *(cont.)*

Diorama

For the last Book Buddy activity, you will design and create a diorama. A diorama is a three-dimensional scene that is constructed inside a small box. For this activity, a shoe box is the perfect size. Everyone in class will assemble his/her own diorama from the Book Buddy idea. This display should prove to be a creative, colorful, and exciting place! Before you begin designing yours, you will need to brainstorm some scenes from this potential book. Take a few moments now and write down at least four brief events, adventures, activities, or times of trouble or happiness that may happen in the story of The _____ and the _____.

Scene	Characters	Setting	Action	Details
1.				
2.				
3.				
4.				

Once you have chosen the scene that you would like to create, you may begin assembling your diorama.

Materials Needed:

- 1 shoebox
- 1 index card 3" x 5"(7.5 cm x 13 cm)
- scissors
- glue and/or tape

- construction paper (all colors)
- colored pens and crayons
- any extras that you feel would make the scene more interesting

Complete an index card for your diorama and glue it to the top so that viewers will get some important information.

> Name of Book:
>
> The _____ and the _____
>
> Author's Name: _____
>
> Characters in This Scene: _____
>
> _____
>
> This is a scene of _____
>
> _____

Unit Test

Matching: Match the vocabulary word with its synonym.

_____ 1. antimacassar	A. steal
_____ 2. momentum	B. essay
_____ 3. predicament	C. angry
_____ 4. incinerator	D. protective cover
_____ 5. incredulous	E. chaos
_____ 6. conscience	F. disbelieving
_____ 7. pandemonium	G. furnace
_____ 8. pilfer	H. unpleasant situation
_____ 9. composition	I. obligation to be good
_____ 10. indignant	J. motion

True or False: Write **T** or **F** next to each statement below.

_____ 1. The Gridley family is from Iowa.

_____ 2. When Ralph first sees Keith, he is very excited about the boy's size.

_____ 3. Ralph falls into the metal wastebasket when the telephone ring scares him.

_____ 4. Ralph and Keith are both surprised that they can speak the same language.

_____ 5. Matt opens the door for Ralph to get back into Room 215 on the night the door accidentally shuts.

_____ 6. Ralph and his family always have plenty of choices when it comes to food, so having room service does not impress them.

_____ 7. Ralph cannot resist finding out whether the motorcycle is stronger than the vacuum cleaner.

_____ 8. Keith makes Ralph a crash helmet from half of a rubber ball.

_____ 9. The night that Keith gets sick, he does not give Ralph's family any food.

_____ 10. Matt finds the motorcycle.

Short Answer: Provide a short answer for each question.

1. Where did Keith's mother want to spend the Fourth of July?

2. How do the motorcycle and ambulance run?

3. Why does Keith forgive Ralph so quickly?

4. Who are Betty and Mary Lou, and where were they from?

5. Why does Ralph decide not to go with Keith back to his home?

Essay: On the back of this paper, respond to the comments in complete sentences.

1. Describe Ralph's plan for taking the aspirin up to Keith's room.

2. Explain the circumstances which lead to Ralph feeling like he is more grown up.

Response

Identify the speakers and explain the meanings of the following quotes from *The Mouse and the Motorcycle*.

Teacher Note: Choose an appropriate number of quotations for your students.

Chapter 1: *"I'm not driving another mile on a California Highway on a holiday weekend."*

"I wouldn't mind a few mice."

Chapter 2: *"You stay away from that telephone cord!"*

Chapter 3: *"If you don't like mice you better stay away from that knothole under the window in room 215."*

Chapter 4: *"Here it is. I wonder how it got there."*

Chapter 5: *"Let me at him!"*

"Nice little machine you got there."

Chapter 6: *"What's the use of having a motorcycle if you can't go tearing around staying out late?"*

"You haven't been associating with people!"

Chapter 7: *"I'll give to you a paper of pins, for that's the way my love begins."*

"Let me down and I'll dig him out!"

Chapter 8: *"That's a young mouse for you . . . Can't take care of anything."*

"I guess I should have known you weren't old enough to be trusted with a motorcycle."

Chapter 9: *"They say I'm in too much of a hurry . . . They say I don't want to take time to learn to do things properly."*

"The housekeeper . . . your Uncle Lester . . . the sheets. Oh, do be quiet, everybody."

Chapter 10: *"Aren't you going to bed pretty early?"*

"I should have thought of it myself . . . I knew we were almost out."

Chapter 11: *"To pilfer a pill . . . An aspirin tablet."*

"Just look at his cunning little paws."

Chapter 12: *"You are a nuisance, that's what you are. A four-footed, hair-covered nuisance."*

"Hey, Keith! I've got it!"

Chapter 13: *"If there is anything I can't stand, it's a cheeky mouse."*

"You grow a little bit every day."

"Then it's settled!" . . . "but first you must ask your mother."

Conversations

Work in groups to write and perform the conversation that might have occurred in each of the following situations.

- Keith and his parents have travelled over the United States for five days in a car. They have driven across plains, mountains, and deserts and ended up at the Mountain View Inn. What might they have talked about as they travelled? (3 people)

- Ralph's mother worried a great deal about Ralph and her children. She worried that there would not be enough food, the hotel would be torn down for the new highway, and, above all, she worried about aspirin. Pretend that Ralph's mother is getting together with a contemporary mother. What would they chat about? (2 people)

- While Ralph was trapped in the metal wastebasket, two ant scouts appeared on the rim. Ralph was embarrassed, and he told them to go away. What would have been their conversation if the ants had stayed? (3 people)

- When Ralph first rode the motorcycle with Keith's permission, Keith instructed him to watch out for his tail so that it would not get caught in the spokes. What other safety tips would Keith have shared? (2 people)

- When Ralph took his first midnight ride out into the hallway, he sped past his Aunt Sissy. She stopped to stare as he waved. If she had gone back to the mousehole where Ralph's mother and brothers and sisters were, what would they all have said? (5–7 people)

- While Ralph was trapped in the pile of dirty linen, the terrier came rushing into the room and began to bark at Ralph. What would Ralph have said back to the dog if he had decided to talk with him? (2 people)

- When Ralph told Keith that he had lost the motorcycle, Keith said that he should have known Ralph was not old enough to be trusted with a motorcycle. Ralph couldn't think of anything to say at this point. What might have their conversation included if they had continued talking? (2 people)

- When all Ralph's relatives became frightened and panicked about the War on Mice by the hotel management, the mousehole became total pandemonium. Ralph decided to take charge of the situation, much to everyone's surprise. Act out the conversations that all the relatives would have had about Ralph's new attitude and his sudden growing up. (5–8 people)

- If the two teachers and Ralph could have spoken the same language, what would they have said to each other as Ralph was trapped under the glass? (3 people)

- When Ralph brought the aspirin back to room 215, Keith's parents thought the night clerk had put it on the night table during the night. If Mr. and Mrs. Gridley could talk with Ralph, what would they all say? (3 people)

Extension: Choose your own conversation idea for the characters in *The Mouse and the Motorcycle*. Write your idea down and ask your teacher if your group could perform this conversation.

Bibliography of Related Reading

Adams, Laurie and Allison Coudert. *Alice and the Boa Constrictor.* (Houghton, 1983).

Angell, Judie. *A Home Is to Share, and Share, and Share.* (Bradbury, 1984).

Baylor, Byrd. *Hawk, I'm Your Brother.* (Macmillan, 1976).

Bunting, Eve. *Jane Maring, Dog Detective.* (Harcourt, 1984).

Burnford, Sheila. *The Incredible Journey.* (Little Paper, 1961).

Byars, Betsy. *The Midnight Fox.* (Viking, 1968).

Campbell, Barbara. *A Girl Called Bob and a Horse Called Yoki.* (Dial, 1982).

Davis, Deborah. *The Secret of the Seal.* (Crown, 1989).

Duncan, Lois. *Hotel for Dogs.* (Avon, 1971).

Eckert, Allan. *Incident at Hawk's Hill.* (Bantam, 1971).

Estes, Eleanor. *Ginger Pye.* (Harcourt, 1972).

Gates, Doris. *A Morgan for Melinda.* (Viking, 1980).

George, Jean Craighead. *The Cry of the Crow.* (Harper, 1980).

Graeber, Charlotte. *Towner Fudge.* (Lothrop, 1987).

Hallstead, William. *Tundra.* (Crown, 1984).

Hart, Dorothy and Paul Mantell. *Animal Orphans.* (Scholastic, 1988).

Hass, Dorothy. *Poppy and the Outdoors.* (Whitman, 1981).

Hass, Jessie. *Keeping Barney.* (Scholastic, 1982).

Hess, Lilo. *The Good Luck Dog.* (Macmillan, 1985).

Kipling, Rudyard. *The Jungle Book.* (Putnam, 1950).

Kjelgaard, James. *Big Red.* (Holiday, 1945).

London, Jack. *White Fang.* (Airmont, 1985).

McInerney, Judith. *Judge Benjamin: Superdog.* (Holiday, 1982).

Morey, Walt. *Gentle Ben.* (Dutton, 1965).

Mowat, Farley. *The Dog Who Wouldn't Be.* (Bantam, 1957).

North, Sterling. *Rascal: A Memoir of a Better Era.* (Dutton, 1984).

Pearce, Philippa. *The Battle of Bubble and Squeak.* (Deutsch, 1976).

Rawls, Wilson. *Summer of the Monkeys.* (Doubleday, 1977).

Royds, Caroline. *The Animal Tale Treasury.* (Putnam, 1986).

Answer Key

Page 10
1. Accept appropriate answers.
2. Room 215, Mountain View Inn
3. Matt is 60 years old and does a variety of jobs at the Inn. He serves as bellboy, room service, and custodian.
4. Mrs. Gridley does not like the Inn. She thinks it is too old, dusty, and probably full of mice.
5. A sedan, a sports car, an ambulance, and a red motorcycle
6. Ralph is disappointed at the size of Keith because smaller children usually leave more crumbs. Then, he feels hopeful because medium-sized boys leave good quality food. He feels joy at seeing the apple core and then despair when Keith's mom tosses it into the wastebasket. Finally, he feels eager, impatient, excited, and curious all at once upon seeing the motorcycle and hearing the motor sound.
7. Ralph's mother worries about him because he is a reckless mouse.
8. The motorcycle is half the length of the cars. It is painted a shiny, red color and has good tires. It has a pair of chromium mufflers and a license plate.
9. Ralph feels something that looks so real has to run.
10. Ralph begins to move his feet across the table top to get the motorcycle to move. The telephone rings suddenly and scares Ralph. He forgets to hit the brakes and is carried off the table and into the wastebasket.

Page 17
1. Accept appropriate answers.
2. One handlebar is bent, and some of the paint is chipped off the rear fender.
3. Uncle Victor accidentally lands in a metal wastebasket and is not able to climb out. No one knows for sure, but it is assumed that he is dumped into the incinerator.
4. Ralph tries running and throwing his body against the side of the wastebasket to tip it over. He tries lifting the apple core onto the motorcycle to use the core as a ladder.
5. Ralph figures that if he stays in the wastebasket, he will end up in the incinerator. If he talks with Keith, he might figure out a way to escape.
6. Keith tells Ralph to make the pb-pb-b-b-b noise while he rides the motorcycle and to hold onto his tail so it will not get caught in the spokes.
7. A dog barks as Ralph rides by room 211.
8. Accept reasonable answers.
9. Matt lets Ralph back into Keith's room.
10. Accept well-written answers.

Page 22
1. Accept appropriate answers.
2. Ralph thinks that wearing clothes must be a nuisance.
3. Ralph's family mostly eats graham and zwieback crackers, bits of candy, an occasional apple core or peanuts, and some toast crust. Their room-service treat is a peanut butter and jelly sandwich.
4. Ralph promises Keith that he will ride the motorcycle only at night.
5. Ralph holds onto the motorcycle and drags himself forward along the bike.
6. Ralph wants to determine whether the motorcycle or the vacuum cleaner is stronger.
7. Ralph decides to leave the motorcycle behind and chews holes only big enough to save his own life.
8. Keith gives Ralph a crash helmet made from a Ping-Pong ball.
9. Keith tells Ralph, "I guess I should have known that you weren't old enough to be trusted with a motorcycle."
10. Accept well-written answers.

Answer Key *(cont.)*

Page 29

1. Accept appropriate answers.
2. Ralph is on the windowsill of Keith's room. He goes there because he wants to be alone to think.
3. Keith decides not to be really angry because he gets into messes too.
4. Ralph's brothers, sisters, and cousins are huddle together in fright. All the relatives are there. Everybody is so upset because the hotel management found out about the mice and is planning to get rid of them.
5. Ralph becomes very calm and clearheaded and knows exactly what his family should do. He takes charge of the situation.
6. Keith becomes sick with a high fever and needs an aspirin.
7. Ralph decides to help Keith because he has been such a good friend, has forgiven Ralph's mistakes, and fed his family.
8. Betty and Mary Lou are elementary school teachers. They both mention their classes.
9. She calls him a pest.
10. Accept well-written answers.

Page 34

1. Accept appropriate answers.
2. He finds an aspirin in a room at the bottom level of the hotel.
3. Ralph hides the aspirin behind the ashtray by the elevator.
4. "Wh-e-e Wh-e-e!" is the sound the ambulance makes.
5. Ralph interrupts the terrier's sleep so he will start barking. His master will open the elevator to take the dog outside, and Ralph will follow.
6. Keith's parents think that the night clerk left the aspirin on the table and that they did not hear him because of the rattling windows.
7. Ralph earns the privilege to go downstairs.
8. Keith learns that growing up is more than just getting physically bigger. It is also about learning responsibility and making wise decisions.
9. Keith likes the thought of Ralph riding the motorcycle. He thinks that maybe one day he might grow up to be trusted with a big one.
10. Accept reasonable answers.

Page 43

Matching		**True and False**	
1. D	6. I	1. F	6. F
2. J	7. E	2. F	7. T
3. H	8. A	3. T	8. F
4. G	9. B	4. T	9. F
5. F	10. C	5. T	10. T

Short Answer

1. Keith's mother wanted to spend the Fourth of July in San Francisco.
2. The motorcycle and ambulance run when the driver makes a special noise.
3. Keith forgives Ralph so quickly because he knows what is was like to make mistakes and be in trouble too.
4. Betty and Mary Lou are school teachers from Wichita, Kansas.
5. Ralph does not go with Keith because he does not want to live in a cage, and he has just earned the privilege.

Essay

Accept answers that contain accurate information.